NEW BLACK

Saints

&

Martyrs

of the 21st Century

Dewalt Missa T

DISCLAIMER NOTIFICATION

Although the author/publisher has made every effort to ensure
that the information in this publication was correct at press time,
the author/publisher don't assume and hereby disclaim any
liability to any party for any loss, damage, or disruption caused by
errors or omissions, whether such errors or omissions result from
negligence, accident, or any other cause. If you won't accept these
conditions, please stop reading this book now and return it. The
author/publisher shall not be liable for any physical, psychological,
emotional, financial, or commercial damages, including, but not
limited to, special, incidental, consequential or other damages. Our
views and rights are the same: You are responsible for your own
choices, actions, results, and consequences. This report is
presented solely for educational purposes. The author/publisher is
not offering it as advice or motivation of any kind. While efforts
have been used in preparing this book, the author/publisher makes
no representations or warranties of any kind and assumes no
liabilities of any kind with respect to the accuracy or completeness
of the contents and specifically disclaims any implied warranties of
merchantability or fitness of use for a particular purpose. The
author/publisher shall not be held liable or responsible to any
person or entity with respect to any loss or incidental or
consequential damages caused, or alleged to have been caused,
directly or indirectly, by the information and/or opinions
contained herein.

ISBN-13: 978-1537304120
ISBN-10: 1537304127

DEDICATION

To all Brothers and Sisters.
Kings and Queens.
Princes and Princesses.
Whose lives have been cut short.
Whose lives have been destroyed.
Whose lives have been changed forever.
The executions and murders stop now.
The violence stops now.
Justice must prevail.

As you read the names and brief stories of
fallen brothers and sisters, remember them as
the true new Black Saints and Martyrs of our
new century. Re-read their stories often.
Shout out their names.
Follow the links and do your own research.
Their names CANNOT be forgotten.

-Dewalt Missa T

FOREWORD

This book is the tragic testament to the state of affairs in America today. As you read the stories of the new Black Saints and Martyrs of the 21st Century, you will probably start to notice disturbing trends and truly sickening similarities.

It isn't just your imagination. It is real. And worst of all, it continues. On and on. All around us.

New Black Saints & Martyrs serves to honor the memories of some of the many Black lives recently cut short by "interactions" with the police.

This book is also intended to start conversations. To be read and re-read often. To open eyes. To be shared with others. To be given to loved ones and to be passed around among friends. To keep us alert. To remind us that these aren't just isolated events. And to encourage us to do our own research and follow the facts, and hold the police accountable.

Carry this book everywhere you go. Let it be seen. Let it be a visible and glaring reminder that we aren't afraid to shine a light on the injustice. No more.

Take it to demonstrations. Wave it high in the air while demanding justice and an end to all the senseless violence. The back cover was specially designed to draw attention at rallies and protests, to promote solidarity as we refuse to forget what has been done to our brothers and sisters, as we speak their names and make their memories permanent.

Let the media see this book. Use it to remind reporters *to be truthful in their reporting* about the circumstances and events surrounding endless police violence and police interactions with Black people.

Make sure the police see this book. Let them know *we know* exactly what's been going down. That the police *need to be held accountable and will be held accountable* for the way *they choose* to interact with the Black people they encounter. Justice will prevail.

Finally, with heavy hearts, we know that there are so many more that need to be remembered. If you have other new Black Saints & Martyrs for consideration for the next edition, please email the details to: NewBlackSaints@outlook.com

And just know how sad it is that us authors *had to choose* to remain anonymous for the real fear of retribution against us, our families and our children. Please respect that.

IMMORTAL WORDS OF BLACK WISDOM

Before the Black Saints & Martyrs section begins, here are some immortal words of Black wisdom, some from many years ago, but still relevant today.

A man dies when he refuses to stand up for that which is *right*. A man dies when he refuses to stand up for *justice*. A man dies when he refuses to take a stand for that which is *true*.

The Rev. Martin Luther King, Jr. speaks from the pulpit Selma, AL, March 8, 1965

You have seen how a man was made a slave; you shall see how a slave was made a man.

Frederick Douglass
Narrative of the Life of Frederick Douglass (1845)

A nation that continues year after year to spend more money on military defense than on programs of social uplift is approaching spiritual death.

Dr. Martin Luther King, Jr.
Where Do We Go from Here: Chaos or Community? (1967)

The press is so powerful in its image-making role, it can make the criminal look like he's the victim and make the victim look like he's the criminal. This is the press, an irresponsible press... If you aren't careful, the newspapers will have you hating the people who are being oppressed and loving the people who are doing the oppressing.

Malcolm X
Speech at Audubon Ballroom in Harlem (December 13, 1964)

In a world filled with hate, we must still dare to hope. In a world filled with anger, we must still dare to comfort. In a world filled with despair, we must still dare to dream. And in a world filled with distrust, we must still dare to believe.

Michael Jackson

Truth is powerful and it prevails.

Sojourner Truth

Our mistreatment was just not right, and I was tired of it.

Rosa Parks

If you hear dogs, keep going. If you see torches in the woods, keep going. If there's shouting after you, keep going. Don't ever stop. Keep going. If you want a taste of freedom, keep going.

Harriet Tubman

You are young, gifted, and Black. We must begin to tell our young: There's a world waiting for you. Yours is the quest that's just begun.

James Weldon Johnson (1894)

Darkness cannot drive out darkness;

only light can do that.

Hate cannot drive out hate;

only love can do that.

Hate multiplies hate,

violence multiplies violence,

and toughness multiplies toughness

in a descending spiral of destruction....

The chain reaction of evil –

hate begetting hate,

wars producing more wars –

must be broken,

or we shall be plunged

into the dark abyss of annihilation.

Dr. Martin Luther King, Jr.
Strength To Love, 1963

BLACK SAINTS & MARTYRS

TANISHA ANDERSON

Cleveland, Ohio

37 years old when she died the night of
November 12-13, 2014

Tanisha was remembered as a straight-A student who aspired to be a broadcast journalist.

Tanisha was "a beloved sister, daughter and friend with a generous streak."[1]

According to court documents filed by Tanisha's family, the family called 911 on November 12, 2014 for help since Tanisha was "having a mental health crisis."[2]

 Tanisha apparently suffered from bipolar disorder and heart disease[3], and had "recently been discharged from the mental hospital and needed to return there to be stabilized."[4]

---

[1]www.theguardian.com/us-news/2015/jun/05/black-women-police-killing-tanisha-anderson

[2] https://assets.documentcloud.org/documents/2796294/Joell-Anderson-affidavit.txt

[3]www.cleveland.com/metro/index.ssf/2015/01/tanisha_anderson_was_restraine.html

[4] https://assets.documentcloud.org/documents/2796294/Joell-Anderson-affidavit.txt

The first set of responding police officers spoke to Tanisha "and she appeared to settle down."[5]

Later, when Tanisha tried to leave home and "was acting disoriented" the family called 911 again.[6]

The second set of responding police officers reportedly "attempted to push her into the zone car and eventually taking her to the sidewalk and leaving her there cold, face down, and not breathing."[7]

Instead of receiving the help she needed, after police intervened, Tanisha died.

There has been no ruling as of yet on police responsibility during this altercation.

However, on January 2, 2015 the Cuyahoga County Medical Examiner's office officially ruled Tanisha's death a homicide, specifically "sudden death associated with physical restraint in a prone position."[8]

---

[5] https://assets.documentcloud.org/documents/2796294/Joell-Anderson-affidavit.txt

[6] https://assets.documentcloud.org/documents/2796294/Joell-Anderson-affidavit.txt

[7] www.wkyc.com/news/local/cleveland/family-of-tanisha-anderson-alleges-cover-up-in-her-death/124729395

[8] www.leveland.com/metro/index.ssf/2015/01/tanisha_anderson_was_restrain e.html

SEAN BELL

Queens, New York

23 years old when he died on November 25, 2006

Sean was remembered as a loving and caring son, father, fiancé, brother, and friend.

Sean met his girlfriend in high school when she was in the 10th grade. They went out for 6 years and were supposed to be married the day Sean died. [9]

With over 100 invited guests, the wedding was scheduled to be held at a fancy restaurant in Ozone Park in Queens, N.Y.

Sean dropped his girlfriend off at her mother's house so she could get ready for her bridal shower that evening. Sean went out to enjoy his bachelor party at a club in Queens. [10]

Leaving the club in the early morning, Sean and his friends got into his car. Suddenly a man approached them holding a gun. Some have speculated Sean thought they were getting carjacked or robbed. The man turned out to be a police officer. As Sean tried

---

[9] http://transcripts.cnn.com/TRANSCRIPTS/0612/04/lkl.01.html
[10] http://transcripts.cnn.com/TRANSCRIPTS/0612/04/lkl.01.html

to drive, five police officers fired about 50 shots into Sean's car.

The police officer who started the shooting claimed to have seen a fourth person in Sean's car with a gun.

No such fourth person was ever discovered.

While Sean's friends in his car were seriously hurt – one had 19 gunshot wounds – Sean was killed. [11]

Instead of celebrating a joyous wedding, Sean's family held a funeral.

---

[11] http://cityroom.blogs.nytimes.com/2008/04/02/doctor-tells-of-a-19-gunshot-wound-survivor/

SANDRA BLAND

Hempstead, Texas

28 years old when she died on July 13, 2015

Sandra "Sandy" Bland, a Chicago native, was known for her "feisty" spirit and "strong" character.

Sandy may be best known for her now-viral Facebook vlog entitled "SandySpeaks." After announcing that "It's time for me to do God's work," Sandy started recording and posting videos on many important and current topics, from racial hostility and police brutality to people missing out on life because they were too engrossed in their smartphones.[12]

During the summer of 2015, Sandy was road-tripping to her new job at Prairie View A&M University. She had graduated from there in 2009, where she was on a prestigious music scholarship, and was reportedly excited and "in good spirits" about the new job and the future. [13]

One day while driving, Sandy was pulled over by a Texas state trooper for "failing to signal when she

---

[12] www.thenation.com/article/what-happened-to-sandra-bland/
[13] bigstory.ap.org/article/f0dff63b60cc4593821efe63cfe84c44/friend-sandra-bland-was-good-spirts-jail-death

changed lanes." [14] During the car stop, the Texas state trooper told Sandy to put out her cigarette which Sandy questioned.

Unbelievably, the situation over the cigarette quickly escalated and Sandy found herself in jail, having been arrested for "assault of an officer." Sandy didn't have enough money to make bail. [15]

Within three days, Sandy was dead.

According to the coroner, Sandy committed suicide by hanging herself in her Waller County Texas jail cell with a plastic garbage bag.

---

[14] highline.huffingtonpost.com/articles/en/sandra-bland-jail-deaths/
[15] highline.huffingtonpost.com/articles/en/sandra-bland-jail-deaths/

REKIA BOYD

Chicago, Illinois

22 years old when she died on March 21, 2012

Rekia Boyd was remembered by her brother as a "young beautiful girl."[16] Her favorite color was yellow, and she carried a yellow purse the night she died.

Rekia was out with some friends. Witnesses said that there were at least 60-70 people hanging out in a park on the West Side of Chicago, enjoying the evening. [17]

At some point, an off-duty Chicago police officer in his Mercedes pulled up to Rekia and her three friends who were hanging out in an alley by his home.

According to authorities, the police officer then "argued with the group over noise." [18]

Moments later, claiming he saw a gun in a young man's hands (it was actually a cellphone), the officer fired 5 shots over his shoulder into the group,

---

[16] www.youtube.com/watch?v=yAeP4FUXSuY
[17] www.youtube.com/watch?v=yAeP4FUXSuY
[18] www.huffingtonpost.com/entry/dante-servin-quits_us_573b7f22e4b0ef86171c6575

wounding the young man and "striking (Rekia) Boyd... in the back of the head." [19]

Although the judge in the case called the officer's actions "so dangerous it is beyond reckless," the judge officially acquitted the officer on a legal technicality.[20]

In the meanwhile, innocent and unarmed, Rekia's life was over.

[19] www.huffingtonpost.com/entry/dante-servin-quits_us_573b7f22e4b0ef86171c6575
[20] fusion.net/story/130482/they-took-the-whole-thing-as-a-joke-why-rekia-boyds-killer-went-free/

RUMAIN BRISBON

Phoenix, Arizona

34 years old when he died on December 2, 2014

Rumain was remembered as a "gentle father of four who was dropping off fast food for his kids at his family's apartment."[21]

According to police, some people told them that drugs were being sold out of an SUV that Rumain was sitting in.

When police went to investigate, Rumain ran away and was chased by a police officer into an apartment.

A struggle ensued.

According to a police officer spokesperson, "During the struggle, Brisbon put his left hand in his pocket and the officer grabbed onto the suspect's hand, while repeatedly telling the suspect to keep his hand in his pocket. The officer believed he felt the handle of a gun while holding the suspect's hand in his pocket."[22]

---

[21] www.washingtonpost.com/news/morning-mix/wp/2014/12/05/how-a-white-phoenix-cop-killed-an-unarmed-black-man/
[22] www.usatoday.com/story/news/nation/2014/12/04/phoenix-police-unarmed-man-killed-by-officer/19878931/

The police officer shot and killed Rumain.

According to the Washington Post, Rumain "was not armed when a police officer fired two bullets, killing him in the presence of his girlfriend and 15-month-old child."

It turned out that *what the officer thought* was a gun "turned out to be a bottle of oxycodone pills."[23]

---

[23] www.usatoday.com/story/news/nation/2014/12/04/phoenix-police-unarmed-man-killed-by-officer/19878931/

MICHAEL BROWN, JR.

Ferguson, Missouri

18 years old when he died on August 9, 2014

Michael Brown was described by friends as a good-natured "gentle giant" and as a "quiet person with a wicked sense of humor."[24]

Known to family and friends as "Big Mike" he "was a big brother to two little sisters and a brother. He had a big smile and at close to 6'4" he seemed bigger than life to those who knew him."[25]

An aspiring rapper, Big Mike had just started recording music at the house of his grandmother. [26]

Just days before he died, Big Mike recorded a song he called "My Pain" featuring the lyrics:

> "Feel my pain. Feel my pain. Smoking Swishers. Feel my pain. Feel my pain. We're the same children Jesus made."[27]

[24]www.slate.com/articles/news_and_politics/politics/2014/11/darren_wilson_s_racial_portrayal_of_michael_brown_as_a_superhuman_demon.html
[25] fox2now.com/2014/08/12/a-look-at-who-was-michael-brown/
[26] fox2now.com/2014/08/12/a-look-at-who-was-michael-brown/
[27] www.dailymail.co.uk/news/article-2730153/A-kid-broken-home-beat-odds-to-college-A-rapper-sang-smoking-weed-feds-A-violent-robbery-suspect-caught-shocking-video-just-real-Michael-Brown.html

On his final day, Big Mike was walking down a Missouri street with a friend after taking some cigarillos from a local convenience store without paying. A police officer noticed the friends who matched the description of the convenience store robbery suspects, pulled over, and a struggle followed.

There were differing versions of what happened but in the end, within three minutes of encountering police, an unarmed Big Mike was shot multiple times and died.[28]

Many weeks of unrest followed.

Even though Attorney General Eric Holder released the official Department of Justice investigation report that found no credible witnesses saying Big Mike had his hands up and said "don't shoot,"[29] the "Hands up - Don't Shoot" rallying cry swept the nation.

---

[28] http://www.bbc.com/news/world-us-canada-28841715

[29] https://www.justice.gov/sites/default/files/opa/press-releases/attachments/2015/03/04/doj_report_on_shooting_of_michael_brown_1.pdf

MIRIAM CAREY

Washington, D.C.

34 years old when she died on October 3, 2013

One of five sisters, Miriam was a dental hygienist with a one-year-old daughter.

The dentist who Miriam worked with for eight years described her as a "non-political person" who was "always happy."[30]

Another co-worker said Miriam was "the sweetest person you ever want to know."[31]

On October 3, 2013, Miriam drove with her 13-month-old daughter from Connecticut to Washington, D.C. No one in her family seemed to know why Miriam had travelled to the nation's capital.

At around 2:13 pm, Miriam drove up to one of the White House security checkpoints. After she passed it, Secret Service officers tried to stop her, but Miriam made a U-turn and drove away.

Police mobilized to pursue her.

---

[30] abcnews.go.com/US/miriam-carey-capitol-suspect-suffered-post-partum-depression/story?id=20465157
[31] www.washingtonpost.com/sf/style/2014/11/26/how-miriam-careys-u-turn-at-a-white-house-checkpoint-led-to-her-death/

After about a seven minute car chase, police stopped Miriam's car and shot into the back of the vehicle, blowing out the rear windshield.

Miriam was hit by 5 of the dozens of bullets fired by police that day and died.

Miraculously, Miriam's daughter was not physically hurt. [32]

After the shooting, Miriam was found to be unarmed and no weapons of any sort were ever found in her vehicle or in her home.

---

[32] www.washingtonpost.com/sf/style/2014/11/26/how-miriam-careys-u-turn-at-a-white-house-checkpoint-led-to-her-death/

PHILANDO CASTILE

Falcon Heights, Minnesota

32 years old when he died on July 6, 2016

Philando worked as a "nutrition services supervisor at J.J. Hill Montessori Magnet School." He was described by co-workers as having a "cheerful disposition" and was a "team player." [33]

Known as a "kind gentle soul," a "quiet man" who loved video games and "driving old cars," Philando was much loved by the children at the school where he worked. [34] [35]

On July 6, 2016, after bringing over takeout from Taco Bell to eat with his sister, Philando left and picked up his girlfriend and her 4-year-old daughter. They shopped at a local grocery store.

Before they got home, Philando was pulled over by St. Anthony police officers. [36]

Apparently the officers thought Philando matched the description of a robbery suspect. [37]

---

[33] www.startribune.com/what-we-know-about-philando-castile/385853331/
[34] www.nytimes.com/2016/07/13/us/philando-castile-minnesota-police-shooting.html
[35] www.startribune.com/outpouring-of-grief-from-philado-castile-s-st-paul-school-community/385892971/
[36] www.nytimes.com/2016/07/13/us/philando-castile-minnesota-police-shooting.html

According to Philando's girlfriend, as the police officers approached the car, one of the officers ordered Philando to get his ID which he tried to do, while Philando also stated he had a legal firearm Philando was licensed to carry.

Suddenly the officer shot Philando multiple times and Philando's girlfriend began broadcasting the scene live on Facebook.

She said, "He let the officer know that he had a firearm and he was reaching for his wallet and the officer just shot him in his arm." [38]

Philando died from his wounds shortly afterwards.

[37] abcnews.go.com/US/cops-thought-philando-castile-robbery-suspect-dispatch-audio/story?id=40439957
[38] www.cnn.com/2016/07/12/us/police-shootings-investigations/

ALEXIA CHRISTIAN

Atlanta, Georgia

26 years old when she died on April 30, 2015

Alexia Christian was the mother of two young boys. Red was her favorite color.

Alexia's aunt remembered her as being "a wild child. She was a sweetie pie. Always a smile. She had the best dimples in the world and you wouldn't do nothing but smile when you see her."[39]

Apparently after being placed in a patrol car following her arrest for suspicion of auto theft, the police allege Alexia escaped from her handcuffs and began shooting at the police officers, who were now both sitting in the front seat, with a stolen gun.

Officers shot Alexia and she died soon thereafter. [40]

According to her mother, the claim that Alexia had stolen a pickup truck was simply "not true." [41]

---

[39] www.wsbtv.com/news/local/family-holds-vigil-victim-officer-involved-shootin/53882831
[40] www.ajc.com/news/news/woman-killed-in-shootout-with-atlanta-police-ident/nk65N/
[41] ww.blackgirltragic.com/home/2016/7/17/2oyfbplap5as6ijtzrcwtznkvr0ua3

Further, while the Christian family sought answers, her grandmother "questioned how police could have bungled a routine arrest, one that cost the life of her granddaughter."[42]

Alexia's mother told the press that "I don't know the truth of what happened. I just know that my daughter was viciously gunned down, you know, like she was a hardened criminal."

She added, "I want to tell law enforcement officers that they are trained to serve and protect, not murder and ask questions, and cover up stuff later."[43]

[42] www.blackgirltragic.com/home/2016/7/17/2oyfbplap5as6ijtzrcwtznkvr0ua3
[43] www.cbs46.com/story/28964795/mother-of-woman-killed-i-shouldnt-be-making-funeral-arrangements

JOHN CRAWFORD III

Beavercreek, Ohio

22 years old when he died on August 5, 2014

John Crawford was the father of two young boys, and had an "infectious sense of humor" and a "quirky laugh." [44]

John's mother told reporters, "I miss him saying 'mom'; I miss his phone calls and his text messages; I miss coming home and seeing that he ate all my food. There's a lot of little things I miss about him. I miss his smile. I miss hearing his voice."[45]

On August 5, 2014, John was shopping in Walmart with his girlfriend. They were headed for a family cookout and wanted to get ingredients for s'mores.

As he walked the isles, John picked up off a shelf, an unpackaged and unloaded BB rifle for sale in Walmart's sporting goods section. He spent the next 5 minutes or so in the pet products aisle speaking on his cell phone with the mother of his two children.

---

[44] www.theguardian.com/world/2014/sep/30/police-officer-shot-john-crawford-walmart-lied-victims-mother-says
[45] www.theguardian.com/world/2014/sep/30/police-officer-shot-john-crawford-walmart-lied-victims-mother-says

As he chatted, he casually held the BB rifle, occasionally swinging it at his side.

Unknown to John, another shopper in Walmart saw him with the BB gun and called 911.

The caller claimed John was pointing the rifle at customers, including children. Police rushed to respond.

Within minutes, John was shot in "the back of the left arm and in his left side" by responding police, and John later died. The autopsy "indicates that he was not facing the officers when he was shot."[46]

Surveillance video showed John never pointed the rifle at police.[47]

---

[46] www.theroot.com/articles/culture/2014/09/witness_in_john_crawford_iii_shooting_changes_story/3/

[47] www.washingtonpost.com/news/the-watch/wp/2014/09/25/mass-shooting-hysteria-and-the-death-of-john-crawford/

MICHELLE CUSSEAUX

Phoenix, Arizona

50 years old when she died on August 14, 2014

Michelle Cusseaux's mother said Michelle was "a lovely person, a giving person who had a mental health problem." [48] Her issues included bipolar disorder, schizophrenia and depression.

Realizing Michelle needed special help and attention on August 14, 2014, Michelle's mother contacted the police for a transport to a mental-health facility.

When the police showed up at Michelle's apartment, something went seriously wrong.

At some point, Michelle is alleged to have attacked police with a hammer. One of the officers shot Michelle and she later died in the hospital. [49]

Speaking to reporters, Michelle's mother summarized it like this, "From what I understand, after pickup orders had been given for the police to go out and pick Michelle up, to bring her in, to get her back on medication, the officers to first arrive

---

[48] www.azcentral.com/story/news/local/phoenix/2014/08/15/phoenix-police-shooting-family-victim-speaks/14148523/
[49] ktar.com/story/91104/police-chief-im-sorry-for-what-happened-to-michelle-cusseaux/

had things under control. And at some point, Michelle was inside, said—her door was open when they appeared. Her front door was open with the screen locked, and Michelle had let them know that she was OK. I guess they were there doing a wellness check. Michelle said she was OK, and 'just go away.' At some point, the sergeant, 17-year sergeant, came on board and overstepped his boundaries. He pried open Michelle's door. He allegedly said she came at him with a hammer. And he shot her at close range once in the heart. So Michelle was killed in her home."[50]

Since then, Phoenix Police demoted the sergeant and have started retraining officers dealing with mental health pickups.

---

[50] www.democracynow.org/2015/5/20/police_killing_of_michelle_cusseaux_ra ises

SHANTEL DAVIS

Brooklyn, New York

23 years old when she died on June 14, 2012

Shantel was remembered as a kind-hearted woman who was "family oriented; she cared for the elderly, sick and disabled. She had strength of character, came from a loving family, was kindhearted, generous and had an enormous heart." [51]

According to the *Shantel Davis Committee for Justice and Beyond*, Shantel was an "unarmed, African American woman was brutally shot and killed by (an) NYPD Narcotics Detective."

On June 14, 2012, after Shantel had run a series of red lights, she crashed an allegedly stolen car into a minivan, and police intervened.

Police shot Shantel once in the chest and Shantel died.[52]

As Shantel's cousin said at her funeral, "She was a decent person. Forget the rumors. Nobody's perfect. Everyone's got a rap sheet."[53]

---

[51] nycal.mayfirst.org/node/6690

[52] www.villagevoice.com/news/the-shantel-davis-story-ignites-protests-in-brooklyn-6681544

Shantel's uncle had similar sentiments saying, "She was no angel, but it's not fair. Kids these days don't have jobs, there's nothing there for them. So they get into trouble." [54]

Shantel's father said he just wanted "justice for my baby. The march will go on until this cop is brought to justice." [55]

[53] www.dnainfo.com/new-york/20120623/east-new-york/family-buries-shantel-davis-amidst-controversy-pain

[54] www.dnainfo.com/new-york/20120623/east-new-york/family-buries-shantel-davis-amidst-controversy-pain

[55] www.dnainfo.com/new-york/20120623/east-new-york/family-buries-shantel-davis-amidst-controversy-pain

PATRICK MOSES DORISMOND

New York, New York

26 years old when he died on March 16, 2000

Patrick was the loving father of two young children. Patrick worked as a security guard in New York City.

Friends called Patrick "easygoing, polite and honest."[56] After his death, Patrick was remembered by his brother Charles Andre– the singer known as *Bigga Haitian* – in a touching reggae song called "Tribute to Patrick Dorismond."[57]

On March 16, 2000, Patrick had completed his security guard work shift and had gone out with a friend to a lounge.

When it was time to go home, Patrick and his friend were minding their own business and standing in front of the lounge waiting for a taxi.

Suddenly, Patrick was approached, and a middle-aged man started asking Patrick where to buy drugs.

Patrick told him "to keep moving."

---

[56] www.nytimes.com/2000/03/17/nyregion/undercover-police-in-manhattan-kill-an-unarmed-man-in-a-scuffle.html
[57] www.youtube.com/watch?v=QL_u55vnU3A

Patrick "did not know that the detectives who approached them – all in plain clothes – were police officers." [58]

The men apparently kept badgering Patrick.

"The situation escalated until Patrick's voice rose, warning the troublemakers to get lost." [59]

Some sort of scuffle ensued and backup police officers jumped in as well.

Almost instantly, one police officer shot unarmed Patrick in the chest and killed Patrick. [60]

[58] www.nytimes.com/2000/03/17/nyregion/undercover-police-in-manhattan-kill-an-unarmed-man-in-a-scuffle.html
[59] www.globalresearch.ca/fifteen-years-ago-the-killing-and-funeral-of-haitian-american-patrick-dorismond-shot-by-undercover-nypd-cops/5437698
[60] www.cbsnews.com/news/no-trial-for-dorismond-shooter/

SHARMEL EDWARDS

Las Vegas, Nevada

49 years old when she died on April 21, 2012

Sharmel was a single mom and a grandmother who worked with children that were disabled. Sharmel was also raising two teen daughters of her own. She is reported to have had "no major criminal history."[61]

On April 21, 2012, Sharmel's boyfriend, a local bar owner, called the Las Vegas police to report that Sharmel had taken his car without permission.

Sharmel was described by friends as being "emotionally distraught. She had had an argument with her boyfriend." [62]

The police found the car and stopped Sharmel but she wouldn't exit the vehicle for about half an hour.

When she did step out, police allege she was holding a gun.

Witnesses told versions of the story that went from Sharmel was holding her hands up, to Sharmel was

[61] www.reviewjournal.com/news/crime-courts/friends-woman-killed-police-was-nonviolent

[62] ebwiki.org/articles/sharmel-edwards

holding a cellphone, to Sharmel held a gun which was found near her body in the aftermath.

In the end, Sharmel was shot by police in a barrage of bullets and died at the scene. [63]

A friend said, "It just didn't seem like Sharmel. I've never known her to be violent at all."[64]

---

[63] www.reviewjournal.com/news/crime-courts/friends-woman-killed-police-was-nonviolent

[64] www.reviewjournal.com/news/crime-courts/friends-woman-killed-police-was-nonviolent

MALCOLM FERGUSON

Bronx, New York

23 years old when he died on March 1, 2000

Malcolm's mother said "Malcolm was my biggest baby." She added that Malcolm "was a loving, happy-go-lucky little boy" who was "always worried about me because I'm legally blind. He was very close to his sisters and brothers because his father died when they were young." [65]

Malcolm had a very close bond with his mother and his siblings, always looking out for them. He was especially protective of his mother.

According to his mother, "Malcolm wanted to be a paralegal to help people after what he witnessed in prison. He felt he wanted to help people who were incarcerated."[66]

When unarmed 23-year-old Amadou Diallo was killed by the NYPD, Malcolm was very upset.

---

[65] http://atlantablackstar.com/2015/01/26/black-lives-matter-profiles-remembering-the-joyful-spirit-of-malcolm-ferguson-killed-after-filing-a-lawsuit-against-the-nypd/
[66] http://atlantablackstar.com/2015/01/26/black-lives-matter-profiles-remembering-the-joyful-spirit-of-malcolm-ferguson-killed-after-filing-a-lawsuit-against-the-nypd/

In fact, less than a week before Malcolm died, Malcolm "had been arrested for protesting the shocking acquittal of four cops who had shot immigrant worker Amadou Diallo 41 times." [67]

On March 1, 2000, only 3 blocks away from the spot where Amadou was shot to death by police, an unarmed Malcolm was shot in the head by a police officer, at very close range, in the hallway of an apartment building. [68] [69]

Malcom died at the scene. [70]

[67] www.workers.org/2010/us/malcolm_ferguson_0318/

[68] http://peoplesjustice.org/case/malcolm-ferguson

[69] www.nydailynews.com/news/crime/pay-mom-10-5m-bronx-death-nypd-told-article-1.223579

[70] http://www.nytimes.com/2000/03/02/nyregion/drug-officer-kills-suspect-in-a-struggle.html

JANISHA FONVILLE

Charlotte, North Carolina

20 years old when she died on February 18, 2015

Janisha was known as a "small, quiet woman who kept to herself" and was "quiet and dependable" at her restaurant job.[71]

Janisha's godmother remembered her as "a sweetheart."[72]

Over the years, Janisha struggled with some mental health issues. She had been diagnosed with "a mood disorder and depression and was once hospitalized for intentionally cutting herself."[73]

On February 18, 2015, Janisha and her girlfriend were apparently arguing much of the day, and Janisha was becoming increasingly emotional.

Around p.m., the girlfriend's sister reportedly called 911 for help with a domestic disturbance at Janisha's home.

---

[71] www.charlotteobserver.com/news/local/crime/article10668737.html

[72] www.twcnews.com/nc/charlotte/news/2015/02/19/family--friends-of-victim-shot--killed-by-cmpd-officer-seeking-answers.html

[73] www.charlotteobserver.com/news/local/crime/article15728675.html

Police were dispatched. [74]

Janisha's girlfriend said she met the police outside, told them Janisha had a knife, "but she was not going to hurt them - she just needed to go to mental health to be evaluated." [75]

Janisha's girlfriend "followed police inside and stayed behind them." [76]

According to police, they found Janisha inside and told her to drop the knife. Police report that Janisha "lunged" at them.[77] Her girlfriend said that Janisha "took one step towards her, without threatening cops."[78]

Within moments, a police officer shot Janisha twice, and Janisha died.

---

[74] www.charlotteobserver.com/news/local/crime/article10783382.html

[75] www.wsoctv.com/news/local/girlfriend-victim-deadly-police-shooting-speaks-ou/52843884

[76] www.charlotteobserver.com/news/local/crime/article10783382.html

[77] www.charlotteobserver.com/news/local/crime/article10668737.html

[78] makheruspeaks.blogspot.com/2015/04/no-chargers-for-officer-who-killed.html

EZELL FORD

Los Angeles, California

25 years old when he died on August 11, 2014

Ezell grew up in South Los Angeles, one of seven children. As a youngster, he showed a natural talent for basketball, so good that he got a scholarship to attend a private school.

Unfortunately, according to his mother, Ezell began to "exhibit signs of the bipolar disorder and schizophrenia" that peaked in his late teen years. [79]

To clear his head, Ezell loved to walk for hours.

The first time he was shot, Ezell was about 20-years-old.

Ezell was shot in the leg while he was an innocent bystander in the middle of a gang gunfight that ended with four dead and at least a dozen more wounded.

Ezell saw a doctor afterwards for his increased emotional distress, and was prescribed medication for bi-polar disorder.

---

[79] www.huffingtonpost.com/julie-bergman-sender/ezell-ford-remembering-hi_b_6678388.html

On August 11, 2014, Ezell was out walking near his home just after sunset when police stopped him to question him.

The police got out of their patrol car and things went seriously bad.

Police claim Ezell made "suspicious actions" and "knocked one officer to the ground." They said Ezell then struggled with them and grabbed for an officer's gun.

Police say they then shot Ezell multiple times and he died. The autopsy showed three shots, including one in unarmed Ezell's back.

But with no other witnesses, the Ford family lives with many unanswered questions in the death of their mentally ill relative.[80]

---

[80] www.dailymail.co.uk/news/article-2890995/Family-unarmed-mentally-ill-man-Ezell-Ford-accuse-LAPD-executing-autopsy-shows-shot-three-times-officers-including-back.html

SHELLY FREY

Houston, Texas

27 years old when she died on December 6, 2012

"Shelly was the perfect mom, perfect friend, perfect daughter," said Shelly's father.

Shelly was from New Orleans, Louisiana but had moved to Houston after Hurricane Katrina.

Shelly was the mother of two young children. Her father said that Shelly "suffered from financial hardship due to his 2-year-old granddaughter's battle with sickle cell anemia."[81]

On December 6, 2012, around 10 pm, Shelly and two friends were shopping in a Texas Walmart. They went to the registers, paid, and left the store.

A security guard, who was an off-duty deputy sheriff, followed them outside where he confronted them. He accused the three friends of shoplifting.

The three friends ran.

The security guard chased them around the parking lot as they got into Shelly's car. In the car with them were also two young children.

---

[81] www.mommyish.com/2012/12/10/shelly-frey-walmart-shoplifting/

The guard "opened the door and commanded them to stop, but the car was placed in drive and moved forward."[82]

The guard then "fired the deadly shot into the car which hit (Shelly) Frey in the neck."[83]

Later Shelly's mother asked "'why couldn't you just shoot the tire, shoot the window? Was it that serious?" Another friend said," What that look like with him shooting with the darn kids in the car? There were kids in the car with them. Why is he shooting at the car? Come on now, that makes him look bad. That don't even look right."[84]

---

[82] www.mydeathspace.com/article/2012/12/11/Shelly_Frey_(27)_was_shot_by _an_off_duty_deputy_after_she_shoplifted_from_Wal_mart

[83] www.dailymail.co.uk/news/article-2245074/Walmart-security-guard-shoots-shoplifting-mother-dead-parking-lot-tries-escape-young-children.html

[84] www.dailymail.co.uk/news/article-2245074/Walmart-security-guard-shoots-shoplifting-mother-dead-parking-lot-tries-escape-young-children.html

KORRYN GAINES

Randallstown, Maryland

23 years old when she died on August 1, 2016

Korryn was a young mother with young children. The daughter of a police dispatcher, she had graduated Baltimore City College and went to Morgan State University for a semester as a political science major.

Korryn left school to get a job and support her young children. A friend said Korryn "had a huge heart, and she was a woman who just wanted the best for her family and for her children."

Korryn's mother remembered Korryn as "forthright, outspoken and could split opinions." Her mother added that Korryn had "always been extremely friendly, outgoing. I can sum it up like this, either you're going to like her or you wouldn't."

Some years before she died, Korryn sued landlords for alleged lead poisoning she said she got from their properties. Her attorney argued that the exposure to lead caused Korryn "neurological impairments" and a loss of "significant IQ points." [85]

---

[85] www.baltimoresun.com/news/maryland/crime/bs-md-korryn-gaines-tuesday-20160802-story.html

On the morning of August 1, 2016, police went to Korryn's home to serve a warrant to her "for failing to appear in court on a March traffic violation and other charges."[86]

Korryn apparently felt threatened and got her shotgun to protect herself and her 5-year-old son who was with her.

During the 5-hour standoff, Korryn streamed live video and content on the internet.

In the end, after a brief gun battle, police shot and killed Korryn, and wounded her 5-year-old son. [87]

[86] www.baltimoresun.com/news/maryland/crime/bs-md-korryn-gaines-tuesday-20160802-story.html
[87] www.vox.com/2016/8/2/12351500/korryn-gaines-baltimore-police-shooting-video

ERIC GARNER

Staten Island, New York

43 years old when he died on July 17, 2014

Eric was known as a gentle giant and a peacemaker. One woman said "He had a hug and a smile for everybody. He was always trying to keep the peace."

Known as "Big E" and "Teddy Bear" to his friends, Eric had 6 children including one starting college. [88]

According to friends, Eric suffered from health problems such as asthma, narcolepsy, and even diabetes.

With a commanding presence at 6' 3" and about 350 lbs., Eric was described by the mother of his 3-month-old daughter as "a great dad -- he's just a warm guy." She added that Eric "was so proud of his daughter -- she's his miracle." [89]

Another friend talking about Eric said, "Everybody that knows him will tell you that he's a wonderful person. I would hug him every day. He was like a big teddy bear."

---

[88] www.yahoo.com/news/friends-man-nyc-chokehold-case-gentle-giant-205839377.html

[89] www.silive.com/news/index.ssf/2014/07/he_was_a_great_dad_says_family.html

On July 17, 2014, Eric was standing in front of a beauty supply store when police approached him and accused him of selling un-taxed loose cigarettes.

Eric responded with "I was just minding my own business. Every time you see me you want to mess with me. I'm tired of it."

As the officers grabbed at him, Eric said, "Don't touch me please."

The police then wrestled Eric to the ground and put him in what was reportedly a chokehold. The whole incident was captured on video.

As Eric lay on the ground, he was gasping "I can't breathe."

Within minutes Eric was dead.[90]

[90] www.nydailynews.com/new-york/man-filmed-eric-garner-chokehold-plea-deal-article-1.2701695

PEARLIE GOLDEN

Hearne, Texas

93 years old when she died on May 7, 2014

Pearlie was a "spry, sharp woman who was known by many people as 'Miss Sulie' and enthusiastically greeted friends with 'Hey, baby! How you doing?'" [91] Others said Pearlie was a "kind matriarch who greeted people as 'honey pie' and 'sweetie pie.'"[92]

On May 7, 2014, Pearlie's nephew had taken Pearlie to renew her driver's license at the Texas Department of Public Safety. Unfortunately, Pearlie failed her test and her driving license was not renewed. She was reportedly very upset.

Pearlie's nephew took Pearlie home and sat on her porch with her.

When Pearlie insisted on getting her keys back, her nephew refused to give the keys to Pearlie since Pearlie was deemed no longer capable of driving.

Pearlie became very upset and went into her house, got her revolver, and went outside.

---

[91] www.dailymail.co.uk/news/article-2623968/Texas-mayor-calls-cop-shot-dead-93-year-old-woman-SACKED.html

[92] www.theeagle.com/news/local/community-seeks-the-truth-behind-death-of--year-old/article_4f5e732e-88d7-5527-89e7-d29b1fdc4508.html

Pearlie's nephew "ran to the side of the house and called police." [93]

When police arrived and told Pearlie to drop the gun, a shootout ensued and Pearlie was struck twice.

Pearlie later died at the hospital.

Pearlie's nephew told the KBTX News 3 that he "dropped to the ground and started to cry after witnessing the shooting. He blames himself for what happened, even though he knew he had no choice but to call police." [94]

Family and friends were outraged. "Even if she did have a gun, she is in her 90s... I don't see her shooting anyone" one person said. [95]

---

[93] www.kbtx.com/home/headlines/Nephew-Pearlie-Golden-Fired-Gun-Twice-258634411.html

[94] www.kbtx.com/home/headlines/Nephew-Pearlie-Golden-Fired-Gun-Twice-258634411.html

[95] www.nydailynews.com/news/national/texas-shoots-death-93-year-old-woman-answering-911-complaint-article-1.1783289

RAMARLEY GRAHAM

Bronx, New York

18 years old when he died on February 2, 2012

Ramarley was remembered by friends and family as "kind and loving," "our go-to guy – if we needed a light bulb to be changed, that's him. Need a stereo hooked up, that's him. If we needed the garbage taken out, that's him too." "There was never a dull moment when he was around — lots of laughter and fun." [96]

On February 2, 2012, Ramarley was walking around his Bronx neighborhood.

Ramarley didn't know that as he passed by a convenience store and innocently adjusted his waistband, Ramarley caught the attention of an NYPD narcotics unit that "took that to mean the 18-year-old had a gun."[97]

The police officers began to follow Ramarley.

Although police said Ramarley ran from them, a surveillance camera shows Ramarley walking along

---

[96] www.dnainfo.com/new-york/20120218/woodlawn-wakefield/ramarley-graham-funeral-draws-hundreds-mourn-teen-gunned-down-by-police
[97] www.huffingtonpost.com/entry/nypd-commissioner-bratton-lied-ramarley-graham_us_56e18716e4b065e2e3d4e81e

calmly and then entering his apartment building. Ramarley's grandmother and younger brother were in the home at that time as well.

Video then shows police running up to the same entrance, guns in hands, and trying to kick in the door.

After they finally were able to get in the apartment, many police officers swarmed into the building.

One police officer, with his weapon drawn, cornered Ramarley in his bathroom.

The police officer claimed that "in response to his mistaken belief that Mr. Graham was reaching for a gun," the officer shot and killed unarmed Ramarley.[98]

There was no gun.[99]

---

[98] www.nydailynews.com/new-york/bronx/no-grand-jury-killed-ramarley-graham-article-1.2556957

[99] www.nydailynews.com/new-york/bronx/no-grand-jury-killed-ramarley-graham-article-1.2556957

OSCAR GRANT III

Oakland, California

22 years old when he died on January 1, 2009

Oscar was a young father with a 4-year-old daughter.[100]

Oscar was "a butcher at an Oakland market and had previously worked at Kentucky Fried Chicken outlets in Berkeley, San Leandro and Hayward. He attended San Lorenzo High School and Mount Eden High School in Hayward until the 10th grade and eventually earned his GED." [101]

At some point on the night of his death, on New Year's Eve 2009, Oscar and four other young black men were detained by police officers investigating a fight on the Bay Area Rapid Transit (BART).

A cell phone video showed the men sitting against a wall. Oscar was handcuffed and lying flat on the ground surrounded by several officers, when one officer shot him in the back.

---

[100] www.racismreview.com/blog/2009/01/07/racism-the-murder-of-oscar-grant-iii/

[101] www.sfgate.com/bayarea/article/BART-shooting-victim-s-family-files-claim-3177160.php

Oscar died shortly thereafter.[102]

One writer called Oscar's death "an execution" and said Oscar "was a peacemaker trying to get everybody to calm down – his friends, the police – who was seen on videotape around the world not struggling, cooperating, who was seen on videotape around the world, his face on the ground, his hands behind his back, as an officer shot him point blank, killing him."[103]

Oscar's mother had encouraged Oscar to take BART instead of driving which she thought would be safer on New Year's Eve.

She credits the Lord with helping her adding, "It takes prayers, family around you to love you, to tell you it's okay, hug you now and then, tell you it wasn't your fault."[104]

---

[102] www.cnn.com/2009/CRIME/01/06/BART.shooting/

[103] http://sfbayview.com/2009/01/oscar-grant-young-father-and-peacemaker-executed-by-bart-police/comment-page-2/

[104] www.finalcall.com/artman/publish/national_news_2/article_8818.shtml

FREDDIE GRAY

Baltimore, Maryland

25 years old when he died on April 19, 2015

Freddie "Pepper" Gray was remembered as a very popular fixture in his neighborhood. He "never had a real job" since friends said he reportedly lived off monthly checks from a lead-paint lawsuit settlement.

People remembered Freddie as "respectful" "comical" and "one of the little happy-go-lucky guys who visited his mom every day."

Friends also added that Freddie made people "laugh with his off-key singing and perpetual smile. He seduced the girls with his 'swag.'"[105]

On April 12, 2015, around 8:40 am, police officers tried to stop Freddie on the street, but Freddie ran.

Police caught up to Freddie a minute later and arrested him. Freddie asked for an inhaler but was ignored. Police put Freddie in a police van.

In less than an hour, the fire department was called for an "unconscious male." Freddie was in "serious

---

[105] www.washingtonpost.com/local/crime/freddie-was-our-family/2015/04/24/662956a2-e9d4-11e4-9a6a-c1ab95a0600b_story.html

medical distress" and was taken to a Shock Trauma unit where he died on April 19.

NPR reported that Freddie "was not secured in the back of the van, which led to 80 percent of his spine being severed."[106]

ABC news reported that Freddie's autopsy "concluded that his death was caused by a 'high-energy' injury to his neck and spine that likely occurred while Gray was in the back of the police van because he didn't have a seat belt on, according to the autopsy. The medical examiner ruled Gray's death a homicide.[107]

---

[106] www.npr.org/sections/codeswitch/2016/04/20/474668796/reflecting-on-the-death-of-freddie-gray-one-year-later

[107] abcnews.go.com/US/anniversary-freddie-grays-arrest-happened/story?id=38334003

KIMANI GRAY

Brooklyn, New York

16 years old when he died on March 9, 2013

Kimani was a tenth grader remembered by his mother as "my angel, and he's my baby." Friends and family said "everybody loved"[108] Kimani and he was "respectful" and "a typical teenager."[109]

On March 9, 2013, Kimani was standing with a bunch of friends in front of his best friend's house having come from a birthday party. They were hanging out.

A witness said "the worst they were doing, laughing out loud and, you know, talking loud. That's about it."[110]

An unmarked police car pulled up to the friends. Kimani reportedly "adjusted his waistband in what the police described as a suspicious manner."[111]

Police claimed that Kimani had a gun.*

---

[108] www.dailymail.co.uk/news/article-2293691/Kimani-Gray-Mother-16-year-old-shot-dead-police-speaks-nights-rioting-Brooklyn.html

[109] www.huffingtonpost.com/2013/03/11/kimani-gray-shot-killed-nypd-cops_n_2852751.html

[110] www.villagevoice.com/news/eyewitness-police-shot-kimani-gray-while-the-16-year-old-was-on-the-ground-6708923

[111] www.nytimes.com/2013/03/11/nyregion/16-year-old-killed-by-new-york-police.html

Moments later, police opened fire and Kimani was hit by bullets seven times, "including three that struck him in the back." [112]

It is alleged that police left Kimani "on the pavement, perceived not to be getting any medical attention for up to 15 minutes." [113]

Kimani was later pronounced dead at the hospital.

*The NYPD later said prints on the gun found at the scene were not Kimani's, nor did they find Kimani's "palm print on the gun." DNA found on the gun was reportedly not from Kimani either. [114]

[112] http://gothamist.com/2013/03/13/kimani_gray_shot_7_times_by_nypd_3.php
[113] www.nydailynews.com/new-york/brooklyn/parents-boy-shot-police-plan-file-wrongful-death-suit-article-1.1337808
[114] www.nydailynews.com/new-york/nyc-crime/witness-teen-killed-cops-brooklyn-hands-article-1.2579528

AKAI GURLEY

Brooklyn, New York

28 years old when he died on November 20, 2014

Akai was from the U.S. Virgin Islands but moved to New York as a youngster. He was living in Brooklyn with his girlfriend and 2-year-old daughter.

Tragically, Akai's stepfather said that the day after Akai died, "he was supposed to surprise the whole family in Florida... That was Mommy's surprise for Thanksgiving... His mother was his queen. You couldn't say anything about his mother, he would wrap you up... He would write poems for Mommy, he would drop off flowers for her. He would call... Akai was the peaceful, loving type. "[115]

On November 20, Akai was visiting his girlfriend and in their apartment house stairwell when he encountered NYPD officers on routine patrol.

Akai was unarmed.

One rookie police officer was reportedly fumbling around in the dark stairwell with a flashlight and his un-holstered gun when he accidentally discharged it.

---

[115] http://nypost.com/2014/11/21/man-killed-by-rookie-cop-planned-to-surprise-mom-in-florida/

The bullet apparently ricocheted off the wall and then struck Akai in the chest.

Akai never had a chance, and died moments later. [116]

An apartment house neighbor called 911 as Akai's girlfriend attempted CPR.

In the meanwhile, the two officers waited over 5 minutes to radio in the shooting and didn't assist with the CPR. The NYC Mayor called the killing a "tragedy." [117]

[116] www.nydailynews.com/new-york/brooklyn/nypd-officer-guns-man-28-brooklyn-housing-project-article-1.2018724
[117] http://newyork.cbslocal.com/2014/11/21/nypd-investigating-fatal-police-involved-shooting-inside-brooklyn-housing-complex/

MYA HALL

Ft. Meade, Maryland

27 years old when she died on March 30, 2015

Friends said Maya was a wonderful person.

A fellow transgender said Maya "was in a halfway house and she wanted to get money to make herself look good, you know, she didn't have the support. She didn't have any money." [118]

Some transgender prostitutes remembered "Hall as a sweet jokester who let others stay in her motel room when she had one, enjoyed dressing in skirts and kidded her friends." [119]

A transgender advocate added that "Mya had a hard life. She just wanted to have a job, a life, a home. Just the simple things." [120]

Early on March 30, 2015, Maya and another transgender woman were partying with a 60-year-old Baltimore man at a motel. When he went to use

[118] www.abc2news.com/news/state/the-story-behind-the-person-shot-at-nsa-headquarters

[119] www.washingtonpost.com/local/crime/baltimores-transgender-community-mourns-one-of-their-own-slain-by-police/2015/04/03/2f657da4-d88f-11e4-8103-fa84725dbf9d_story.html

[120] www.washingtonpost.com/local/crime/baltimores-transgender-community-mourns-one-of-their-own-slain-by-police/2015/04/03/2f657da4-d88f-11e4-8103-fa84725dbf9d_story.html

the bathroom, Maya and her friend took his car keys and drove off with his SUV.

For unknown reasons, Maya drove the SUV to the restricted part of the NSA headquarters at Ft. Meade. Some believe it was just an innocent wrong turn.[121]

A guard ordered Maya to leave but Maya allegedly sped up headed for a police vehicle.

NSA Police opened fire at the SUV, killing Maya and wounding her passenger.[122]

[121] www.baltimoresun.com/news/maryland/crime/bs-md-nsa-shooting-no-charges-20150623-story.html

[122] www.chicagotribune.com/news/nationworld/chi-nsa-shooting-20150401-story.html

DONTRE HAMILTON

Milwaukee, Wisconsin

31 years old when he died on April 30, 2014

Dontre seems to have struggled with mental health issues for a while. According to Dontre's mother, Dontre was schizophrenic. But she said he had been "doing well, living in group housing and working."[123]

Then, the winter before Dontre died, problems with health insurance resulted in Dontre missing medication. "Had he had that medication, he might still be sitting here with us," said Dontre's mother.[124]

Dontre's mother told police that "the mobile mental health evaluators found Dontre, and told her 'Dontre didn't seem like he was going to harm himself or anyone else, so they let him stay at his residence.'"[125]

On April 30, 2014, in the afternoon, someone at a coffee store called police after seeing Dontre sleeping in Milwaukee's Red Arrow Park.

---

[123] www.dailymail.co.uk/news/article-2809119/Milwaukee-family-seeks-charges-police-shooting.html
[124] www.dailymail.co.uk/news/article-2809119/Milwaukee-family-seeks-charges-police-shooting.html
[125] http://fox6now.com/2014/12/24/documents-describe-dontre-hamiltons-battle-with-mental-illness-his-familys-efforts-to-get-him-help/

Police checked him out and left Dontre alone.

Someone called police again, and police told the caller that Dontre wasn't doing anything wrong.

Unaware of the multiple checks, a third police officer then picked up a voice mail directing him to check out Dontre. When he arrived at the park, he found Dontre lying down on the ground.

The officer helped him up and spoke to Dontre while starting to pat him down.

Suddenly the encounter escalated into some sort of a struggle, and the officer shot Dontre 14 times killing Dontre.[126]

[126] http://archive.jsonline.com/news/milwaukee/autopsy-planned-thursday-on-man-shot-by-police-at-red-arrow-park-b99260307z1-257512561.html

ERIC COURTNEY HARRIS

Tulsa, Oklahoma

44 years old when he died on April 2, 2015

Eric was described by his 16-year-old son as "Sweet, nice, forgiving, thoughtful. He would do anything for anybody."[127]

According to his uncle, Eric "had such an outgoing personality, great heart and big sense of humor. He was really close to his brothers. It's hard to believe he is gone. It hurts so much to think of the tragedy in which he lost his life and the pain my nephew suffered until he took his last breath."

Another person added that, "You were and will always be my definition of a true friend. You constantly amazed me with your steadfast loyalty, giving heart, and endless energy." [128]

On April 2, 2015, Eric was caught up in an undercover police sting operation. Eric was running from the scene when a 73-year-old volunteer reserve sheriff's deputy shot unarmed Eric in the

---

[127] www.newson6.com/story/28778121/tulsa-county-sheriffs-office-releases-video-of-deputy-involved-shooting

[128] www.kennedycares.com/obituaries/Eric-Harris-3/

back as he was apparently lying on the ground at his feet after being tackled by a regular deputy. [129] [130]

Eric died soon thereafter.

A year after his death, Eric's brother said, "He accomplished a lot in his death, I think even more than in his life." Then he added, "I'mma miss my brother, but you know, we all have a destination."[131]

[129] www.usatoday.com/story/news/nation/2015/04/13/oklahoma-shooting-video/25702233/
[130] www.cnn.com/2016/04/27/us/tulsa-deputy-manslaughter-trial/
[131] www.nydailynews.com/news/crime/tulsa-volunteer-deputy-found-guilty-of2nd-degree-manslaughter-article-1.2616920

MEAGAN HOCKADAY

Oxnard, California

26 years old when she died on March 28, 2015

Meagan was in kindergarten when she first heard the story of Pollyanna, and it reportedly became her favorite book. She also fell in love with the song "Polly Wolly Doodle" which inspired her nicknames *Polly Wolly* and *Paulina*.[132]

In high school, Meagan and her sister were chosen to be captains of their cheerleading squads. [133]

When her baby sister was born, she was handed straight to Meagan by the doctor and Meagan and her sister instantly formed an unbreakable bond.

Meagan herself had three wonderful little daughters.[134]

Shortly after midnight on March 28, 2015, Meagan's boyfriend "called 911 requesting police officers to respond to a domestic dispute he was having with" Meagan.[135]

---

[132] www.garciamortuaryoxnard.com/memsol.cgi?user_id=1555412
[133] www.garciamortuaryoxnard.com/memsol.cgi?user_id=1555412
[134] www.garciamortuaryoxnard.com/memsol.cgi?user_id=1555412
[135] www.keyt.com/news/woman-killed-in-oxnard-officer-involved-shooting/32066036

The first police officer on the scene reported hearing screaming, then was met at the door by Meagan's boyfriend.

Seconds later, Meagan reportedly approached with a knife in her hand and the police officer shot and killed Meagan. [136]

Meagan's "three children witnessed the shooting and are with family, following a Child Protective Services evaluation."[137]

---

[136] http://losangeles.cbslocal.com/2015/03/28/knife-wielding-woman-fatally-shot-by-officers-in-oxnard/

[137] www.bet.com/news/national/2015/04/01/meagan-hockaday-shot-and-killed-by-police.html

DARRIEN HUNT

Salt Lake City, Utah

22 years old when he died on September 10, 2014

Darrien was described as "a child at heart... He was the nicest kid, and would never have hurt anyone." Darrien was also "very bright... kind of shy but giving and loving." The family further said Darrien "had a strong desire to serve his country in the Marine Corp and unfortunately never got that chance." [138]

According to friends and relatives, earlier in life Darrien had missed out on some things so when he recently went to a boy scout camp, Darrien "was fun to hang out with... he wanted to try it all, he wanted to learn, he wanted to have experiences that he hadn't had."[139]

Another friend likened Darrien to Jesus Christ.[140]

Darrien's mother also told the media that "My son is a tender heart who would not hurt anybody. Just wanted to be loved."[141]

---

[138] www.theguardian.com/world/2014/sep/17/darrien-hunt-police-shooting-family-friends-remember

[139] www.theguardian.com/world/2014/sep/17/darrien-hunt-police-shooting-family-friends-remember

[140] http://archive.sltrib.com/story.php?ref=/sltrib/news/58425294-78/hunt-darrien-family-scivally.html.csp

On the morning of September 10, 2014, Darrien's relatives said he was "cosplaying — or costumed role playing — as a cartoon character and carrying a sword that was not a weapon, but a costume accessory with a rounded blade."[142]

Someone called 911 and police responded.

Reportedly only moments after police spoke with Darrien, Darrien was dead.

Darrien was shot multiple times from the back as he apparently ran for his life while being chased and shot at by police.[143]

[141] www.dailymail.co.uk/news/article-2756016/Police-deny-race-role-man-s-shooting-autopsy-reveals-shot-behind.html

[142] www.sltrib.com/news/2933436-155/darrien-hunts-mother-says-she-turned

[143] www.msnbc.com/msnbc/darrien-hunt-carrying-toy-sword-shot-and-killed-utah-police

KATHRYN JOHNSTON

Atlanta, Georgia

88 years old when she died on November 21, 2006

Kathryn lived alone in Atlanta and was "so afraid of crime in the neighborhood that she wouldn't let neighbors who delivered groceries for her come into her home." [144]

Kathryn was remembered by a friend as a "sharp, caring woman who was 'like a mother' to her. Johnston never forgot birthdays, addresses or how much she spent at the grocery store each month."

"She was the strongest person I've ever known. People would come in town to visit me, and I would say 'You've got to meet Miss Johnston. She's a phenomenon,'" Kathryn's friend said in a eulogy. [145]

Kathryn's friend added that "this woman didn't bother anyone. She was scared. She stayed in her house. She wouldn't even come to the door for me unless I called first." [146]

---

[144] www.cnn.com/2006/US/11/27/atlanta.shooting/index.html
[145] www.washingtonpost.com/wp-dyn/content/article/2006/11/28/AR2006112800822.html
[146] www.nytimes.com/2006/11/23/us/23atlanta.html

Around 6 p.m. on November 21, 2006, Kathryn was at home when she heard people trying to break into her home, ripping at her burglar bars for a few minutes and smashing her front door.

Terrified, Kathryn got her rusty old revolver and shot at the door, but hit no one.

Suddenly, about half a dozen police officers began shooting back and killed Kathryn in a hail of bullets.

Kathryn was the innocent victim of another botched police drug raid.[147]

Worse, police officers planted drugs in Kathryn's home and made a false statement in an attempt to cover-up their mistakes. Their guilt was eventually uncovered and three police officers went to prison.[148]

[147] www.alternet.org/story/51151/documents_reveal%3A_cops_planted_pot_on_92-year_old_woman_they_killed_in_botched_drug_raid
[148] www.cnn.com/2009/CRIME/02/24/atlanta.police/

AIYANA MO'NAY STANLEY–JONES

Detroit, Michigan

7 years old when she died on May 16, 2010

Aiyana loved to listen to Justin Bieber. [149] And Aiyana liked "Disney's 'Hannah Montana' show and all the Disney princesses."[150]

Aiyana was remembered as "a girl both bossy and sweet, tomboy and girlie-girl, a self-described princess." Her grandmother remembered her as "a beautiful, beautiful angel."

Aiyana's grandmother also spoke of Aiyana's natural rhythm and appreciation for music, "My goodness, the baby was 6 months old, and she could rock herself. She'd rock the boat. It was amazing that a 6-month-old baby could rock like that."

One of her school teachers said that Aiyana "adored her father, because whenever he came to pick her up, she was ready to go, she was right there." The teacher also said that Aiyana "always wanted to

---

[149] www.essence.com/news/hot_topics_4/aiyana_jones_funeral_today.php
[150] www.cleveland.com/nation/index.ssf/2010/05/al_sharpton_tells_girls_mourne.html

make sure that she got her name on the board ... or a star on her paper." [151]

Just after midnight on May 16, 2010, Aiyana's father was walking around their apartment as Aiyana was soundly asleep on the coach and her grandmother watched TV.

Police looking for a murder suspect in another apartment in the same house mistakenly entered Aiyana's home.

Police SWAT officers, accompanied by a reality TV film crew, exploded a flash-bang grenade and then burst into the room.

Within seconds, a police officer fired his submachine gun once, shooting Aiyana in the head killing her. [152]

---

[151] https://presbytera.wordpress.com/2015/01/22/aiyana-monay-stanley-jones/

[152] www.yourversion.com/index.php?p=viewpage&url_id=10836381

KENNY LAZO

Long Island, New York

24 years old when he died on April 12th, 2008

Kenny was a union construction worker and father of a young son.

Kenny was remembered as a good father who had a good heart. [153] Kenny "wasn't afraid to share and show love," someone who "always brought everybody together." [154]

On April 12, 2008, Kenny was driving on the Southern State Parkway.

At some point Kenny was pulled over for speeding, reportedly only 8 miles over the speed limit. [155]

Police claimed that when Kenny struggled with them, they beat and choked Kenny with their flashlights.

After the beating, instead of taking Kenny to the hospital, police took Kenny to a police precinct "where he collapsed." Later, under deposition at

---

[153] www.youtube.com/watch?v=g4Naf9vNMbk
[154] www.youtube.com/watch?v=cg-tmT8JqFA
[155] www.youtube.com/watch?v=cg-tmT8JqFA

trial, the police told many versions of what they claimed happened. [156] [157] [158]

An independent autopsy that the family paid for, reportedly showed that Kenny had been beaten when handcuffed and lying with his face on the ground.[159]

After a long delay, an ambulance was finally called. But it was too late. Kenny was found dead on the floor of the police precinct. [160]

The County Coroner eventually released an autopsy that ruled Kenny's death to be a homicide.

To date, no police officer has been held accountable.

The family feels the whole system is "corrupt," suspects racism, and seeks justice for Kenny. [161]

---

[156] www.newsday.com/long-island/suffolk/wounds-tell-story-of-kenny-lazo-s-death-1.521568?pts=435618

[157] www.themilitant.com/2015/7916/791657.html

[158] https://justiceforkenny.org/kenny/the-murder/

[159] https://justiceforkenny.org/kenny/the-murder/

[160] www.youtube.com/watch?v=g4Naf9vNMbk

[161] www.youtube.com/watch?v=g4Naf9vNMbk

ANTONIO MARTIN

Berkeley, Missouri

18 years old when he died on December 23, 2014

Antonio was described as "like any other kid who had dreams or hopes. We loved being around him. He'd push a smile out of you."[162]

Antonio's father said that "in the last year, he was really trying to find who he was. He was ready to take the world on. He knew he had parents who loved him. He had that support."[163]

Antonio's grandmother said, "When he was around me, he knew to do right." [164]

On the night before Christmas Eve, December 23, 2014, Antonio was outside a gas station convenience store, walking around, and talking to another young man.

[162] www.stltoday.com/news/local/crime-and-courts/parents-of-antonio-martin-say-his-fatal-shooting-doesn-t/article_fdcc9659-905c-5472-b5dd-66f5d36c6fba.html

[163] www.stltoday.com/news/local/crime-and-courts/parents-of-antonio-martin-say-his-fatal-shooting-doesn-t/article_fdcc9659-905c-5472-b5dd-66f5d36c6fba.html

[164] www.stltoday.com/news/local/crime-and-courts/parents-of-antonio-martin-say-his-fatal-shooting-doesn-t/article_fdcc9659-905c-5472-b5dd-66f5d36c6fba.html

Video footage showed the two walking off the lot when a police officer pulled up and got out of his vehicle to approach the two young men.

Moments later, the police officer fired three shots at Antonio. [165]

Police later claimed that Antonio had a loaded gun but that it had not been fired.[166]

Antonio was pronounced dead on the scene by paramedics. [167]

[165] www.theguardian.com/us-news/2014/dec/30/antonio-martin-police-shooting-missouri
[166] www.nytimes.com/2014/12/25/us/berkeley-missouri-police-shooting.html
[167] www.washingtonpost.com/news/post-nation/wp/2014/12/30/police-multiple-witnesses-say-antonio-martin-pulled-gun-on-officer/

TRAYVON MARTIN
Sanford, Florida

17 years old when he died on February 26, 2012

Trayvon was remembered as "an athletically-inclined teen with an eye towards aviation." He is said to have taken an English Honors class although math was reportedly his favorite subject. [168]

Trayvon's mother said Trayvon "had been so looking forward to going to his junior prom, and he had already started talking about all the senior activities in high school."[169]

On February 23, 2012, Trayvon let the house he was staying at to go purchase Skittles brand candy and Arizona brand watermelon fruit juice. [170]

On his walk home, Trayvon was chatting away on a cell phone with his girlfriend. It was drizzling so Trayvon put up the hood on his hoodie. [171]

---

[168] www.biography.com/people/trayvon-martin-21283721#early-life
[169] www.tampabay.com/news/publicsafety/crime/trayvon-martin-a-typical-teen-with-dreams-of-flying-or-fixing-planes/1221425
[170] www.local10.com/news/zimmerman/evidence-trayvon-martins-arizona-brand-watermelon-juice
[171] http://bigstory.ap.org/content/amid-evidence-cache-martin-case-questions-nag

At some point during his return trip, Trayvon was followed and then confronted by a neighborhood watch volunteer.

During the confrontation, Trayvon was shot in the chest and died on the scene. [172]

President Obama said, "I send my thoughts and prayers, as well as Michelle's, to the family of Trayvon Martin, and to remark on the incredible grace and dignity with which they've dealt with the entire situation. I can only imagine what they're going through, and it's remarkable how they've handled it… You know, when Trayvon Martin was first shot I said that this could have been my son. "[173]

---

[172] www.tampabay.com/news/publicsafety/crime/trayvon-martin-a-typical-teen-with-dreams-of-flying-or-fixing-planes/1221425
[173] www.whitehouse.gov/the-press-office/2013/07/19/remarks-president-trayvon-martin

LAQUAN MCDONALD

Chicago, Illinois

17 years old when he died on October 20, 2014

Laquan was a tall teen with a flair for rapping and dancing.

Laquan was remembered by his high school teacher who said Laquan "would come up every morning and hug me, and he would do that with a lot of teachers. He really liked being here... He was a really funny kid. The things he would say were hilarious." [174]

Laquan went through his childhood living with relatives or in foster care homes.

Most recently Laquan was living with his uncle while "his mother was petitioning the court for custody."[175]

On the evening of October 20, 2014, Laquan was walking on a street in Chicago when he was confronted by police who claimed Laquan was holding a knife and threatening them.

---

[174] www.chicagotribune.com/news/ct-laquan-mcdonald-profile-met-20151125-story.html

[175] www.chicagotribune.com/news/ct-laquan-mcdonald-profile-met-20151125-story.html

A police dash cam video revealed that Laquan was apparently walking away from police.

Of the eight police officers at the scene, only one officer started shooting.

Although it seems Laquan fell to the ground after being hit by the first bullet, the police officer kept shooting and Laquan suffered a total of 16 bullet wounds within seconds.[176]

Laquan "still had a pulse when paramedics arrived but was declared dead at the hospital." [177]

[176] www.nytimes.com/2016/08/19/us/laquan-mcdonald-chicago-police.html

[177] www.bbc.com/news/world-us-canada-34917287

NATASHA MCKENNA

Alexandria, Virginia

37 years old when she died on February 8, 2015

Natasha was the mother of a 7-year-old daughter. Natasha's autopsy report said that Natasha had "a well-documented history of major mental illness. Her first psychiatric hospitalization occurred when she was 14 years old.

In the ensuing years Natasha accrued numerous psychiatric diagnoses including: schizophrenia, bipolar disorder and depression."[178]

Natasha called 911 in late January 2015 to report being the victim of an assault. Police responded and at the hospital, Natasha made the decision to drop the assault investigation and no longer wanted any police assistance.[179]

Afterwards, police discovered an outstanding warrant for Natasha and placed her in jail.

While in jail awaiting transfer to another jurisdiction, Natasha's mental health deteriorated and "staff at

---

[178] www.fairfaxcounty.gov/news/2015/report_of_investigation_of_in-custody_death.pdf

[179] www.washingtonpost.com/local/crime/woman-was-restrained-masked-before-death-at-jail/2015/02/19/cf7c731c-b786-11e4-aa05-1ce812b3fdd2_story.html

the jail had become alarmed." Yet the delays to move Natasha went on.[180]

When police finally decided to transport Natasha, the mentally ill woman struggled for about 15-20 minutes with "five deputies in biohazard suits who shocked her four times with a stun gun before she lost consciousness."[181]

Natasha was taken to the hospital where she was declared brain dead.

Natasha "was removed from life support and died on February 8." [182]

---

[180] www.washingtonpost.com/local/crime/woman-was-restrained-masked-before-death-at-jail/2015/02/19/cf7c731c-b786-11e4-aa05-1ce812b3fdd2_story.html

[181] www.dailymail.co.uk/news/article-3229754/Sheriff-releases-video-struggle-inmate-died.html

[182] www.washingtonpost.com/news/local/wp/2015/04/13/the-death-of-natasha-mckenna-in-the-fairfax-jail-the-rest-of-the-story/

GABRIELLA NEVAREZ

Citrus Heights, California

22 years old when she died on March 2, 2014

Gabriella was known as "Gabby" to her family and friends.

Gabby was a young mother with a 3-year-old son who was remembered by her girlfriend as loving her family very much – "That was the most important thing to her, her family."[183]

A family member told the media that Gabby "was taking Prozac and other medications to treat mental illness, and that she hadn't been getting much sleep." The family member added that Gabby "had her problems but we always knew she would outgrow them if she had a chance. But she didn't get the chance." [184]

On March 2, 2014, Gabby and her grandmother had a disagreement and Gabby rode off in her grandmother's car.

---

[183] http://elixher.com/lesbian-woman-of-color-killed-by-sacramento-county-police-officers/
[184] http://fox40.com/2014/03/03/community-mourns-woman-killed-in-officer-involved-shooting/

Gabby's grandmother said she called police to report that Gabby had taken her car.

Using electronic tracking, police located Gabby and the car.

During the ensuing pursuit, police ended up cornering Gabby and shooting at least 14 times into the car, killing unarmed Gabby.

Gabby's grandmother said that Gabby "was very loved. They took her out. Just like that. Just like an animal. And she wasn't any animal. She's my heart. She's always been my heart."[185]

---

[185] http://fox40.com/2014/03/09/grandmother-of-woman-shot-by-police-speaks-out/

DANTE PARKER

Victorville, California

36 years old when he died on August 12, 2014

Dante was the well-respected and loving father of five kids – four daughters and a son. Dante worked for over a decade as a pressman at a local newspaper.

Co-workers remembered Dante as "a big teddy bear," "part of our family," and "a family man" who loved music. [186]

Dante's wife remembered Dante as being "everything to us." She also said that Dante was "the spirit of the house. We would stay up and wait for him to come home. Movie nights on Fridays. He was the best." [187]

On August 12, 2014, Dante was riding a bicycle on the street in Victorville, California.

Police confronted Dante and questioned him about an attempted home burglary.

---

[186] www.nydailynews.com/news/national/father-5-dies-tased-police-arrest-article-1.1904577

[187] www.sbsun.com/government-and-politics/20140819/naacp-calls-for-accountability-in-dante-parkers-police-custody-death

The confrontation turned into a struggle during which time a police officer shot an unarmed Dante with a Taser gun and shocked Dante "between 25 and 27 times." [188]

A second officer "helped handcuff" Dante and "place him in the backseat of a patrol unit, when they saw that he was sweating and breathing heavily." Dante was taken to the hospital. [189]

Shortly afterwards, Dante was pronounced dead, only a few days before his 37th birthday.

---

[188] www.sbsun.com/general-news/20150129/dante-parkers-family-files-lawsuit-over-victorville-mans-in-custody-death

[189] www.nbclosangeles.com/news/local/Man-Dies-in-Deputies-Custody-After-Being-Hit-With-Taser-271144901.html

JERAME REID

Bridgeton, New Jersey

36 years old when he died on December 30, 2014

Jerame was remembered by his wife as "my best friend, my soulmate. The man that promised to love me indefinitely and beyond is gone ... they took him from his family." Jerame's wife added that Jerame was "destined to be someone great, if given a chance ... And they took him from me." [190]

Jerame's mother said that she "will continue to protest to keep Jerame's spirit alive... until justice is achieved — by any means necessary."

On December 30, 2014, Jerame and another man were in a car driving around in New Jersey. Jerame was the passenger.

They were pulled over "allegedly for not making a complete stop at a stop sign."[191]

All caught on dash cam video, police can be heard ordering Jerame to remain in the car after one

---

[190] www.nj.com/cumberland/index.ssf/2014/12/wife_of_man_fatally_shot_by _bridgeton_police_says_my_biggest_fear_has_come_true.html

[191] www.themilitant.com/2016/8002/800251.html

officer "recovered what appeared to be a gun from the vehicle's glovebox." [192]

One police officer recognized Jerame and yelled, "Hey Jerame, you reach for something you're going to be (expletive) dead!"[193]

When Jerame "gets out of the car with what appear to be his hands in front his chest,"[194] police "opened fire, killing him."[195]

[192] www.theguardian.com/us-news/2015/aug/23/jerame-reid-police-shooting-federal-civil-rights-investigation

[193] http://jimfishertruecrime.blogspot.com/2015/04/the-jerame-reid-police-shooting-case.html

[194] www.nj.com/cumberland/index.ssf/2015/01/watch_authorities_release_dashcam_footage_in_bridg.html

[195] www.nbcphiladelphia.com/news/local/Jerame-Reid-Police-Shooting-Grand-Jury-No-Indictment-Bridgeton-322600052.html

TAMIR RICE

Cleveland, Ohio

12 years old when he died on November 23, 2014

Tamir was remembered as living "a beautiful, awesome life of 12 years because his parents, his extended family ... raised him to know beyond a reasonable shadow of a doubt that his life had a purpose, value and meaning." [196]

Tamir was also "praised for his budding talents and described as a popular child who liked to draw, play basketball and perform in the school's drum line."[197]

On November 22, 2014, Tamir and his sister were playing in a park down the block from their home.

Tamir enjoyed sitting on the swings, walking around a gazebo, throwing snowballs, and playing around with a toy gun that a friend had lent to him.

At some point, someone called 911 from the park and reported things like "there's a guy in here with a pistol, it's probably fake, but he's like, pointing it at

---

[196] www.nbcnews.com/news/us-news/tears-funeral-cleveland-boy-tamir-rice-shot-cop-n260741

[197] www.nbcnews.com/news/us-news/tears-funeral-cleveland-boy-tamir-rice-shot-cop-n260741

everybody... it's probably fake... I don't know if it's real or not... (he's) probably a juvenile..." [198]

Police responded. Surveillance cameras captured what happened next.

Tamir was hanging out by a park gazebo. Police quickly pulled up to Tamir and within seconds of getting out of the patrol car, one officer shot Tamir.

Video shows the officers left Tamir to lie on the ground bleeding. [199] Tamir died the next day in the hospital.

Tamir "never pointed a gun at a cop. He wasn't given the chance to even put his hands up."[200]

[198] www.latimes.com/nation/nationnow/la-na-nn-tamir-rice-911-call-20141126-htmlstory.html

[199] https://thinkprogress.org/what-everyone-should-know-about-the-police-killing-of-tamir-rice-2002-2014-370a8340c090#.xb8a8vnct

[200] www.gq.com/story/tamir-rice-story

TAMON ROBINSON

Brooklyn, New York

27 years old when he died on April 18, 2012

Tamon worked at a coffee and muffin shop in Brooklyn[201] and also had a business selling scrap construction materials.

Tamon's mother remembered Tamon as "a good son, never got into any trouble. He never was involved in drugs or gangs. He was friendly; it was rare that he ever got angry with anyone. He was a hard worker and was trying to go to college."[202]

Tamon's manager at work said that Tamon was "hardworking, friendly, got along with everyone."[203]

On April 12, 2012, Tamon was reportedly picking up some discarded paving stones that Tamon "had permission from the building's management to take." [204] [205]

---

[201] www.nytimes.com/2014/08/09/nyregion/city-settles-suit-in-death-of-man-hit-by-a-police-car.html

[202] http://thepeoplesrecord.tumblr.com/post/25378977956/nypd-takes-the-life-of-another-black-male-june-18

[203] https://socialistworker.org/2012/06/18/another-son-taken-by-the-nypd

[204] https://socialistworker.org/2012/06/18/another-son-taken-by-the-nypd

[205] www.streetsblog.org/2012/04/23/tamon-robinson-of-brooklyn-chased-and-killed-by-nypd-officers-in-cruiser/

Police responded to a call "that a man was stealing paving stones." Police chased Tamon, and an initial police report said a police car hit Tamon.[206]

The police later claimed that Tamon "ran into" their cruiser and then fell backwards striking his head.[207]

Witnesses said Tamon was "run over" by police.

Tamon was taken to the hospital where he lay handcuffed to his bed in a coma.

Six days after his encounter with the NYPD, Tamon was taken off life support and died.[208]

[206] www.nytimes.com/2012/04/21/nyregion/man-hit-by-police-car-at-bayview-houses-in-brooklyn-dies.html

[207] www.huffingtonpost.com/2013/04/23/tamon-robinson-nypd-car-grand-jury_n_3139943.html

[208] http://thepeoplesrecord.tumblr.com/post/25378977956/nypd-takes-the-life-of-another-black-male-june-18

TONY TERRELL ROBINSON

Madison, Wisconsin

19 years old when he died on March 6, 2015

Tony was remembered as "a passionate and compassionate young man, and a wonderful friend. He was always there when you needed him for an ear to listen, a deep conversation about life's complexities or just to make you smile."[209]

Tony was also described as "a good, kind-hearted kid, who was happy... he just wanted to be loved."[210]

And Tony was a "big gentle giant."[211]

On March 6, 2015, Tony's friends reportedly called the police for help after noticing that Tony was "behaving in a way that warranted help from an outside source. So the police were called and were notified that, 'Look, my friend here is having a hard time. Maybe he took something.'"[212]

---

[209] www.nbcnews.com/news/us-news/tony-robinson-shooting-more-1-000-attend-funeral-slain-teen-n323626

[210] www.nbcnews.com/news/us-news/slain-teen-tony-robinsons-uncle-says-family-trusts-investigators-n320286

[211] www.nydailynews.com/news/crime/madison-police-told-tony-robinson-assaulted-2-people-article-1.2141789

[212] www.democracynow.org/2015/5/13/wisconsin_activists_to_continue_protests_after

Police were dispatched and one officer confronted Tony in an apartment.

In the ensuing struggle, the police officer shot unarmed Tony multiple times.

Tony died soon after at the hospital.

A family member said "Tony is not a victim. He's our own martyr, a champion of change. And for you I will always stand."[213]

[213] www.cbsnews.com/news/mourners-pack-funeral-for-tony-robinson-madison-wisconsin-teen-killed-by-police/

WALTER SCOTT

North Charleston, South Carolina

50 years old when he died on April 4, 2015

Walter was a U.S. Coast Guard veteran and the loving father of four children.[214]

Family remembered Walter as "one of the nicest people you could meet" who adored his fiancé.

Another family member said Walter "was the best uncle. He used to baby sit me and take me for rides in his car and I'd listen to his old school music like Marvin Gaye and we'd dance along... He was a very loving man and I can't find the words to describe how it feels to see that video. I am in shock." [215]

Walter's mother added that "From a child he has been raised in the church. From day one he sang in the choir, he played the drums he would call his mom every single day. They never got in trouble

---

[214] http://bigstory.ap.org/article/d67e289fc6a64c2896365719826a294b/white-sc-officer-charged-murder-shooting-black-man

[215] www.dailymail.co.uk/news/article-3031108/You-took-Walter-Hysterical-fianc-e-torn-away-Walter-Scott-s-body-lay-lifeless-grass-shot-dead-white-South-Carolina-cop.html

they had a beautiful childhood and I had no problem." [216]

On April 4, 2015, Walter was out driving his new car when police pulled him over reportedly for a "routine traffic stop for a broken brake light."

At some point Walter and the police officer were involved in some sort of scuffle and the police officer shot and killed Walter.

An eye-witness released a cellphone video that showed the shooting and that the police officer had shot Walter multiple times in the back as Walter was running away from him. [217]

---

[216] www.dailymail.co.uk/news/article-3031108/You-took-Walter-Hysterical-fianc-e-torn-away-Walter-Scott-s-body-lay-lifeless-grass-shot-dead-white-South-Carolina-cop.html

[217] www.nytimes.com/2015/04/08/us/south-carolina-officer-is-charged-with-murder-in-black-mans-death.html

ALBERTA SPRUILL

New York, New York

57 years old when she died on May 16, 2003

Alberta was remembered as a kind and loving church-going woman who worked for almost three decades for New York City at the Division of Citywide Administrative Services. [218]

Alberta was a loving grandmother "known for handing out bags of candy to neighborhood children"[219] and was known as "Miss Alberta" by neighbors and friends. [220]

In the early morning hours of May 16, 2003, Alberta was in her apartment and dressing for work.

Just after 6 a.m., as Alberta was getting ready to leave for her job, heavily armed NYPD officers used a battering ram to break down her door.

Police then threw a flash grenade into Alberta's apartment. [221]

---

[218] www.nytimes.com/2003/05/17/nyregion/woman-dies-after-police-mistakenly-raid-her-apartment.html
[219] www.workers.org/ww/2003/harlem0605.php
[220] www.poormagazine.org/node/1334
[221] http://nypost.com/2003/05/30/anatomy-of-nypds-tragic-bad-raid-blunder-in-harlem/

Within moments, the police had handcuffed a terrified and stunned Alberta and started to search her apartment.

At this point, police reportedly realized they had made a mistake and had raided the wrong address.

It was too late for Miss Alberta who began having problems breathing. Alberta told police she had a heart condition and began fading fast.

An ambulance arrived at 6:40 a.m. and got to Harlem Hospital at 7:28 a.m. At some point, Alberta went into cardiac arrest.

At 7:50 a.m., Alberta was pronounced dead. [222]

[222] http://nypost.com/2003/05/30/anatomy-of-nypds-tragic-bad-raid-blunder-in-harlem/

TIMOTHY STANSBURY, JR.

Brooklyn, New York

19 years old when he died on January 24, 2004

Timothy was remembered as a hard-working young man who was working in a restaurant and planning to go to community college.

Timothy was also reported to have wanted to marry his girlfriend. Timothy's mother said that Timothy was "a good child, a respectable young man." Family often called him Tim-Tim.[223]

Timothy's mother added that Timothy "was so against gun violence, he and his friend decided to make a documentary on guns in their neighborhoods before he was killed." The anti-gun documentary is called "Bullets in the Hood: A Bed-Stuy Story." A few months into the documentary's production, Timothy was shot to death by a police officer. [224]

The documentary won the 2005 Sundance Film Festival Grand Jury Prize in Short Filmmaking.

On January 24, 2004, Timothy went to a friend's house to get some CDs and return to a party.

---

[223] www.nytimes.com/2007/05/24/nyregion/24settles.html

[224] http://blackandbrownnews.com/bbn-special-reports/inner-city-blues-timothy-stansbury-1984-to-2004/

Timothy was unarmed and taking a familiar shortcut on his apartment building's rooftop stairwell.

Timothy reached the doorway about the same time as two police officers on rooftop patrol.

One of the police officers, who was carrying his gun in his hand, claimed to be startled by Timothy.

The police officer fired one shot that struck Timothy in the chest. [225]

Timothy was taken to the hospital where he was operated on but there was nothing the surgeons could do.

Eventually Timothy lost his life, about an hour and a half after having been shot.[226]

[225] www.nytimes.com/2007/05/24/nyregion/24settles.html

[226] www.nytimes.com/2007/05/24/nyregion/24settles.html

PHILLIP WHITE

Vineland, New Jersey

32 years old when he died on March 31, 2015

Phillip was the young father of two children and was remembered as his mother's " 'gentle giant' the man who shoveled snow outside her home, loved her meals of potato salad and fried chicken, and joked with her on the deck where they often spent sunny afternoons together."

Phillip was remembered as a "caring person" and "he always was the type to protect you."[227]

Phillips mother added that she "raised Phillip to be a good Christian, and awakened him and his brother, Paige, when they were young by blasting gospel music."[228]

On March 31, 2015, Phillip reportedly had "an 'altercation' with several men. Someone then called 911 with a disorderly person report, saying that the

---

[227] www.nbcphiladelphia.com/news/local/2nd-Cell-Video-of-Police-Interaction-Ahead-of-Vineland-NJ-Phillip-White-298631621.html

[228] http://articles.philly.com/2016-05-05/news/72835408_1_police-officer-medical-examiner-autopsy

caller heard someone "freaking out... going crazy... screaming." [229]

Police responded quickly and aggressively.

One cell phone video apparently shows Phillip "lying face down and not struggling after he was hit multiple times by a police officer sitting on his back."

Later the cell phone video "also appears to show... the police dog running up and biting (Phillip) White."[230]

Phillip was taken to the hospital where he was pronounced dead.

[229] www.pressofatlanticcity.com/news/breaking/no-indictment-for-officers-in-vineland-death-in-custody/article_2aa5db64-34c9-11e6-aa70-fb16a30c86da.html
[230] www.pressofatlanticcity.com/news/breaking/no-indictment-for-officers-in-vineland-death-in-custody/article_2aa5db64-34c9-11e6-aa70-fb16a30c86da.html

TARIKA WILSON

Lima, Ohio

26 years old when she died on January 4, 2008

Tarika was the devoted and good parent of six young children. [231]

A family member said Tarika was a "stay-at-home mother who 'took care of kids and went to bingo.'"[232]

Days after she died, Tarika was supposed to have started college "to study business in hopes of making a better life for herself and her six children."[233]

On January 4, 2015, just after 8 p.m., police looking for a male "suspected drug dealer" in Ohio conducted a raid on Tarika's house. Police detonated "at least one stun grenade." SWAT officers entered the house and arrested the suspected drug dealer. At some point, police shot two dogs downstairs. [234]

When police went upstairs where Tarika and her six children had been cleaning their bedrooms, the violence escalated.

---

[231] www.mapinc.org/drugnews/v08/n039/a01.html
[232] www.mapinc.org/drugnews/v08/n020/a04.html
[233] www.mapinc.org/drugnews/v08/n020/a03.html
[234] www.mapinc.org/drugnews/v08/n020/a04.html

One officer opened fire into Tarika's bedroom.

Tarika was shot and killed by police and police "wounded the year-old baby she held in her arms."[235] [236]

"Two people were shot for no reason. You don't kill innocent bystanders. You don't shoot people for no reason" said a relative. [237]

One writer described the killing noting "unarmed and not suspected of any crimes, Tarika died of her wounds while her child survived."[238]

[235] http://usatoday30.usatoday.com/news/nation/2008-08-04-ohio_N.htm
[236] http://blog.cleveland.com/metro/2008/01/lima_shooting_leaves_the_town.html
[237] www.mapinc.org/drugnews/v08/n020/a02.html
[238] https://tyrantwatch.co/2016/02/16/miss-australia-left-disfigured-because-police-threw-a-flashbang-grenade-into-her-bed-as-she-slept/

OUSMANE ZONGO

New York, New York

43 years old when he died on May 22, 2003

Ousmane was remembered as a "quiet, gentle man who worked tirelessly to send money to his family in" Africa[239] where Ousmane had a wife and two young children he supported.

Ousmane worked in New York City repairing African artifacts and artwork.

A friend said that Ousmane did not like confrontation, "wouldn't challenge anyone" and even lacked the "the nerve to hound customers who owed him money."[240]

On May 22, 2003, Ousmane was innocently working at his art workbench in a building in New York City. In that same building, a company suspected of distributing pirated CDs and DVDs was being investigated by the NYPD. Ousmane had nothing to do with the crooked business.[241] [242]

---

[239] www.democracynow.org/2003/5/27/as_outrage_mounts_in_new_york

[240] www.nytimes.com/2003/05/24/nyregion/friends-recall-a-gentle-reliable-man.html

[241] www.democracynow.org/2003/5/27/as_outrage_mounts_in_new_york

[242] www.complex.com/pop-culture/2013/01/a-recent-history-of-nypd-brutality/ousmane-zongo

NYPD officers had raided the suspected bootleg company and a plainclothes police officer disguised as a post office worker was "monitoring a bin of CDs when he saw Zongo turn on a light."

According to the NY District Attorney's office, the plainclothes police officer allegedly pulled out his gun to challenge Ousmane, but not his badge. [243]

Ousmane, apparently terrified, tried to run away from the man with the gun.

After a brief chase, the plainclothes officer cornered unarmed and innocent Ousmane and shot Ousmane "four times, two of the shots hitting him in the back."[244]

Ousmane died from these bullet wounds.

[243] www.nydailynews.com/archives/news/guilty-immigrant-slaying-beats-manslaughter-charge-article-1.618186
[244] www.complex.com/pop-culture/2013/01/a-recent-history-of-nypd-brutality/ousmane-zongo

MAY YOU ALL

REST

IN

PEACE